MS Access

Davinder Singh Minhas

RISING SUN

RISING SUN
an imprint of
New Dawn Press

NEW DAWN PRESS GROUP
New Dawn Press, Inc., 244 South Randall Rd # 90, Elgin, IL 60123
e-mail: sales@newdawnpress.com
New Dawn Press, 2 Tintern Close, Slough, Berkshire, SL1-2TB, UK
e-mail: ndpuk@newdawnpress.com
          sterlingdis@yahoo.co.uk

New Dawn Press (An Imprint of Sterling Publishers (P) Ltd.)

A-59, Okhla Industrial Area, Phase-II, New Delhi-110020
e-mail: sterlingpublishers@touchtelindia.net
          Ghai@nde.vsnl.net.in

Printed at Sterling Publishers Pvt. Ltd., New Delhi

Contents

Contents

1. Introduction

Microsoft Access is a database software. A database is a collection of data organized in a manner that allows access, retrieval and use of that data. In a manual database, you might record data on paper and store it in a filing cabinet. Database software, like Access, is a software that allows you to create, access and manage a database. Using a database software, you can add, change and delete data in the database; sort and retrieve data from the database; and create forms and reports using the data in the database.

In Access, a database consists of a collection of tables, organized in rows and columns. A record is a row in a table that contains information about a given person, product or event. A field is a column in a table that contains a specific piece of information within a record.

The most ubiquitous of databases is the phone book. The phone book contains several items of information viz, name, address, phone number, etc of each phone subscriber in a particular area. In the database, each subscriber's information will be saved in the same format.

In database phrase, the phone book is a table which contains a record of each subscriber. Each subscriber record contains three fields: name, address, and phone number. The records are sorted alphabetically by the name field, which is called the key field.

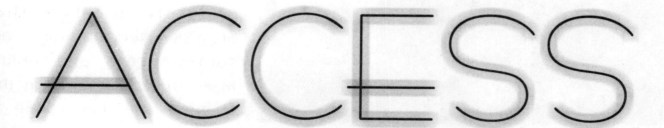

Starting Access

Windows must be running to start Access. You can perform the following steps to start Access:

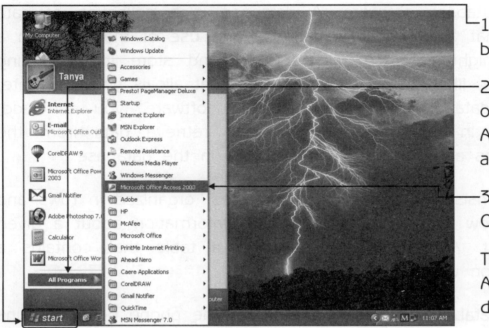

1. Click on the Start button.

2. Point to All Programs on the start menu. The All Programs submenu will appear.

3. Click on Microsoft Office Access 2003.

The Microsoft Office Access 2003 window is displayed.

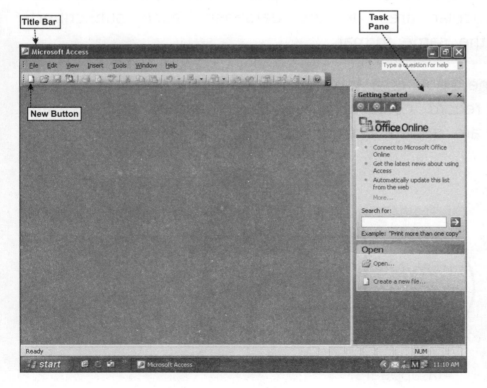

In this picture, the screen gives you a view of the Access window just after the first installation of Access.

You will also notice that a task pane is displayed on the screen. A task pane is a separate window that enables users to carry out some Access and online tasks more efficiently. In this chapter, the task pane is used only to create a new database.

Creating Database Using a Wizard

You can create a complete database by using the Database Wizard that includes at least one table and usually one or more data entry forms and reports. You may want to examine these components to learn more about how they are constructed. You will probably discover that they provide a very useful learning tool. Using the Database Wizard gives you a big head start on the process and you can always modify the wizard-created database later, once you are more familiar with Access.

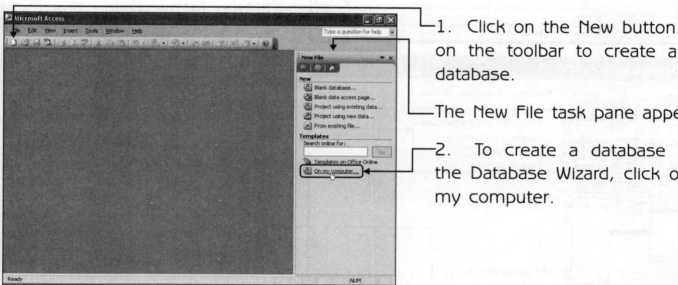

1. Click on the New button ( ) on the toolbar to create a new database.

The New File task pane appears.

2. To create a database using the Database Wizard, click on On my computer.

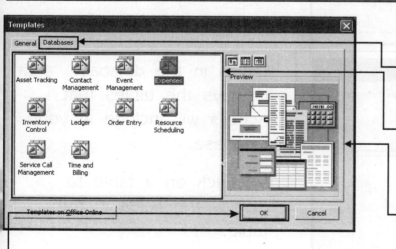

The Templates dialog box appears.

3. Click on the Databases tab in the Templates dialog box.

4. Click on the template that best describes the type of information you want to store.

This area displays a preview of the template you have selected.

5. Click on the OK button to create the database.

The File New Database dialog box appears.

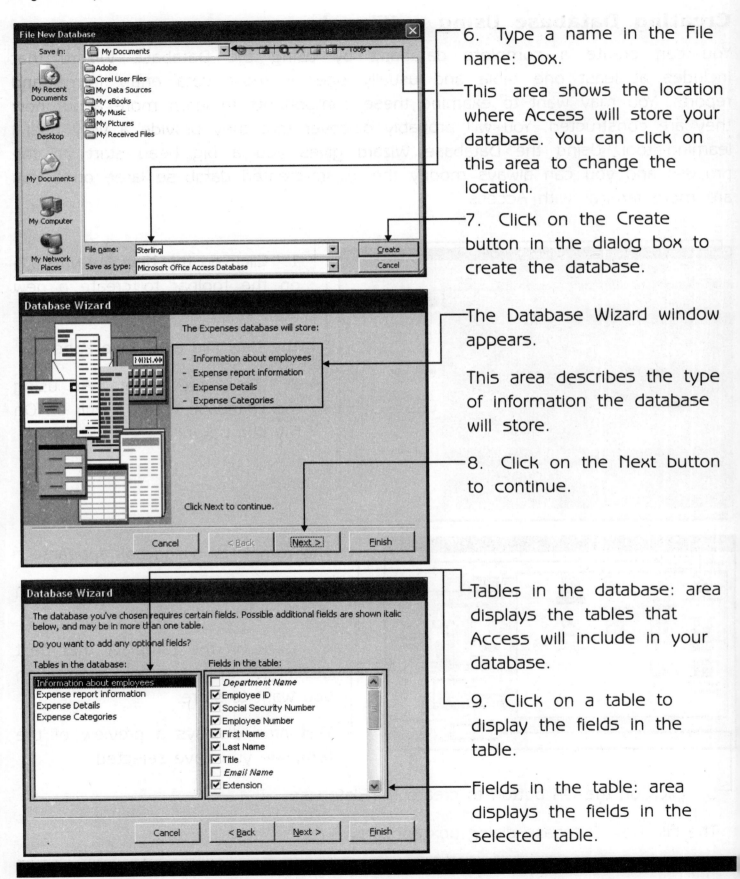

6. Type a name in the File name: box.

This area shows the location where Access will store your database. You can click on this area to change the location.

7. Click on the Create button in the dialog box to create the database.

The Database Wizard window appears.

This area describes the type of information the database will store.

8. Click on the Next button to continue.

Tables in the database: area displays the tables that Access will include in your database.

9. Click on a table to display the fields in the table.

Fields in the table: area displays the fields in the selected table.

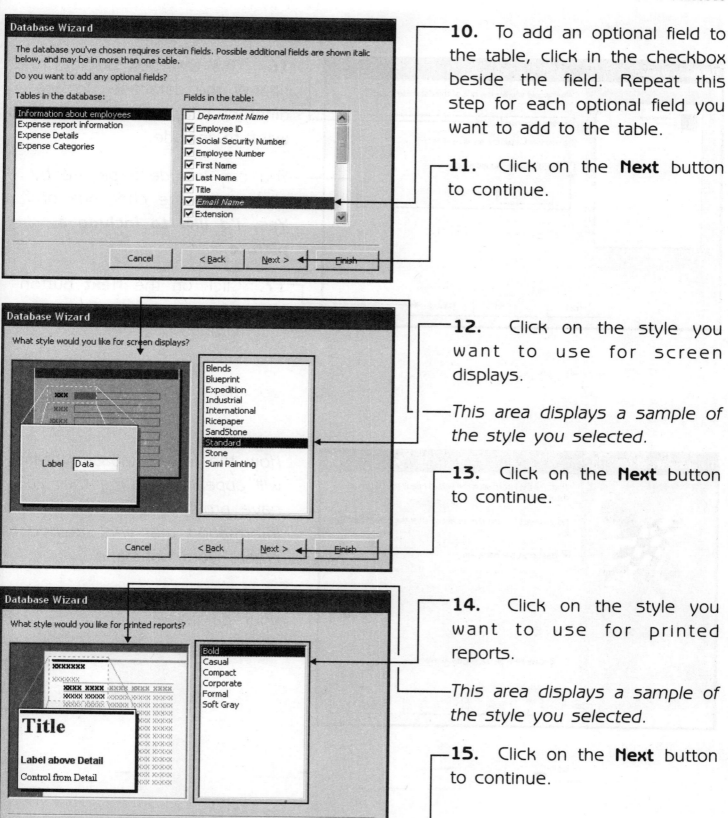

10. To add an optional field to the table, click in the checkbox beside the field. Repeat this step for each optional field you want to add to the table.

11. Click on the **Next** button to continue.

12. Click on the style you want to use for screen displays.

This area displays a sample of the style you selected.

13. Click on the **Next** button to continue.

14. Click on the style you want to use for printed reports.

This area displays a sample of the style you selected.

15. Click on the **Next** button to continue.

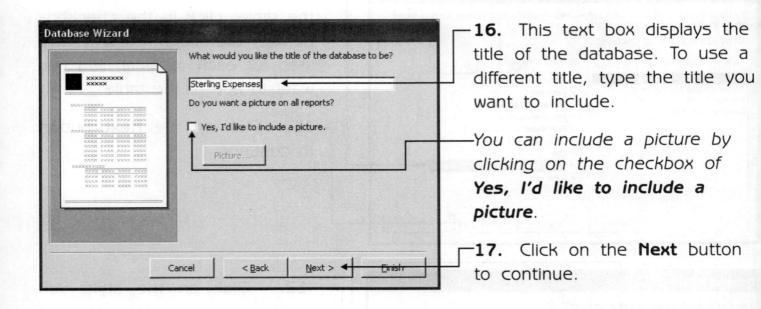

16. This text box displays the title of the database. To use a different title, type the title you want to include.

You can include a picture by clicking on the checkbox of **Yes, I'd like to include a picture**.

17. Click on the **Next** button to continue.

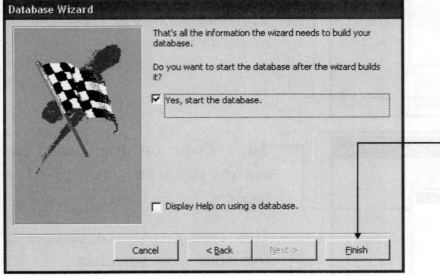

Now the last Database Wizard will appear indicating that you have provided all the information that was needed to create your database.

18. Click on **Finish** to create your database.

Access will create the objects for your database, including tables, forms, queries and reports.

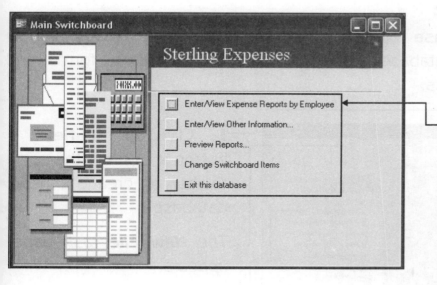

*The **Main Switchboard** window appears which helps you perform common tasks.*

19. Click on the task you want to perform.

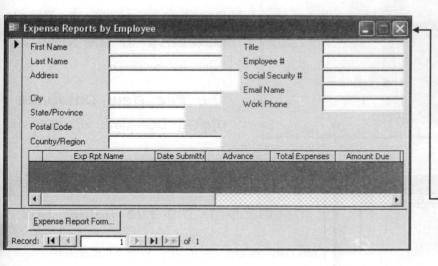

The database object that allows you to perform the task appears.

*If more tasks appear, repeat step **19** to display a database object.*

20. When you finish using the object, click on the **Close** button (x) to close the object and return to the main switchboard window.

2. New Database

Creating a New Database

You can use the **Blank Database** option in the task pane to create a new database. A single file called Database stores all the tables, reports, forms and queries created by you in Access.

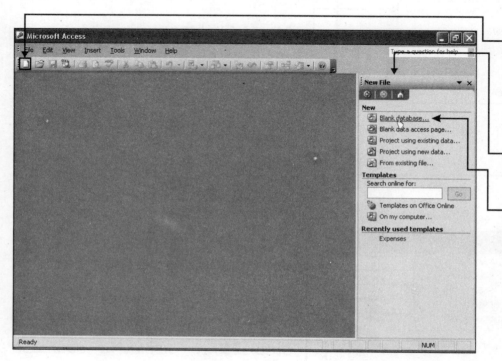

1. Click on the **New** button (▯) on the toolbar to create a new database.

*The **New File** task pane appears.*

2. To create a Blank Database, click on **Blank Database** in the New File task pane.

*The **File New Database** dialog box will appear.*

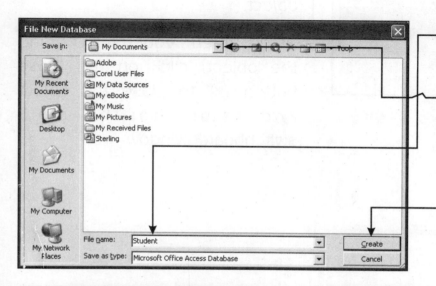

3. Type a name for the database in the **File name:** box.

This area shows the location where Access will store your database. You can click on this area to change the location.

4. Click on the **Create** button to create the database.

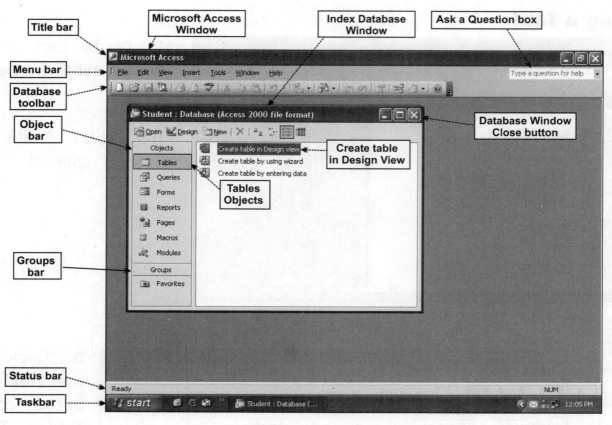

The **Index** database is created and displayed on the desktop.

⦿ The **Title bar** is the first bar on the desktop. It displays the title of the window.

⦿ The **Menu bar** is the second bar containing a list of menu names. To open a menu from the menu bar, click on the menu name.

⦿ The **Database toolbar** is the third bar. The Database toolbar contains buttons that allow you to perform certain tasks faster than using the menu bar. A picture or icon is contained in each button which depicts its function.

⦿ The **Status bar** is placed immediately above the Windows taskbar. It contains special information that is appropriate for the task on which you are working. Currently, it contains the word, Ready, which means Access is ready to accept commands.

⦿ The **Taskbar**, located at the bottom of the screen, displays the Start button, the current time and any program that is running.

Creating a Table

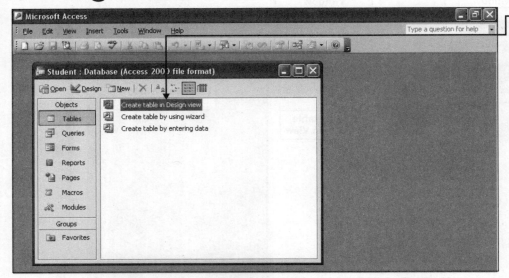

1. Double-click on **Create table in Design view**.

The Table1 : Table Window appears.

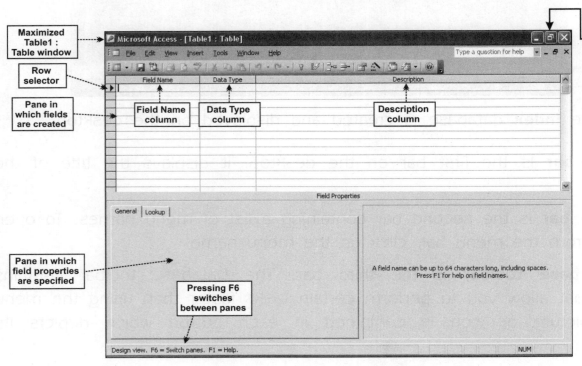

3. Click on the **Maximize** button of **Table1 : Table** window.

You should define the fields by specifying the required details in the Table window to proceed to the next step in creating the table. You should make entries in the **Field Name**, **Data Type** and **Description** columns and then enter additional information in the **Field Properties** box in the lower portion of the Table window.

To create a table, you will be required to describe the **structure** of the table to Access by describing the fields within the table. For each field, you need to fill the following information:

Field name — There must be a unique name for each field in the table. For example, in a Customer table, the field names are Customer ID, Name, Address, City, Country, Telephone and E-mail.

Data type — The type of data to be contained within the field is indicated by **data type**. Some fields can contain only numbers. Others, such as Amount Paid and Current Due, can contain numbers and dollar signs. Still others, such as Name and Address, can contain letters.

Description — You can enter a detailed description of the field in Access.

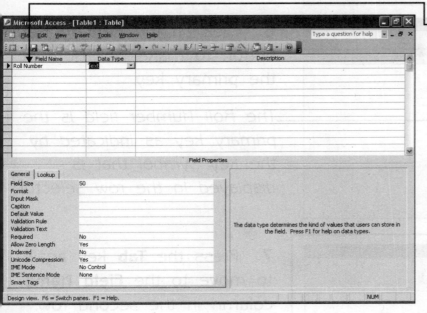

1. Type the name, like Roll Number, in the **Field Name** column.

2. Press the **TAB** key on the keyboard to bring the Insertion point to **Data Type** column.

The words 'Roll Number' display in the Field Name column and the insertion point advances to the Data Type column, indicating that you can enter the data type.

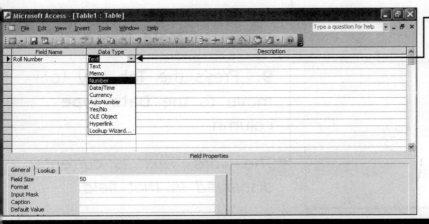

3. If you want to change the data type, click on the down arrow button and change the data type according to your need.

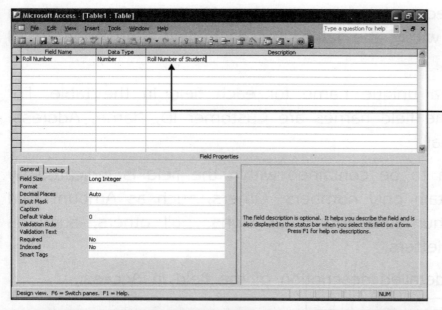

4. Press the **TAB** key to move the insertion point to the **Description** column.

5. Type in the **Description** column.

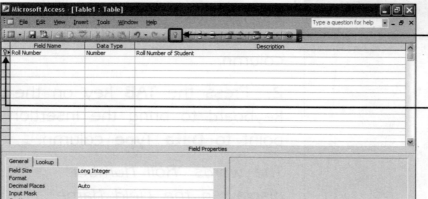

6. Click on the **Primary Key** button to make Roll Number the primary key.

The Roll Number field is the primary key as indicated by the key symbol that is displayed in the row selector.

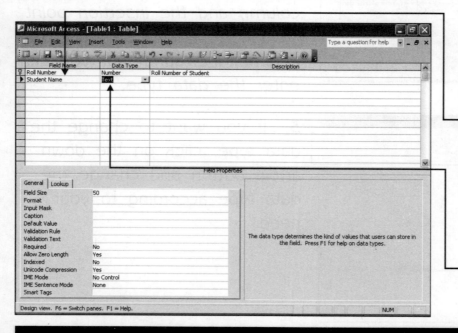

7. Press the **Tab** key again to move to the **Field Name** column in the second row.

8. Type the text (Student Name) in **Field Name** column.

9. Press the **Tab** key to move to the **Data Type** column.

The word 'Text' is currently displayed in that field.

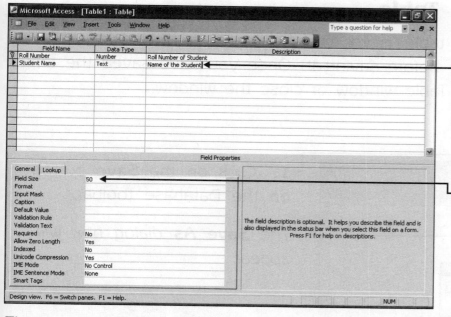

10. Press the **Tab** key to move the insertion point to **Description** column, if you want the Data Type as **Text**.

11. Type the text for the **Description** column.

12. To move the insertion point to the **Field Size** Property box, press the **F6** key on the keyboard.

The current entry in the Field size property box (50) is selected.

13. Type any size you want, for eg, **20**, as the field size. Press the **F6** key to return to the Description column for the Student Name field and then press the **TAB** key to move to the **Field Name** column in the third row.

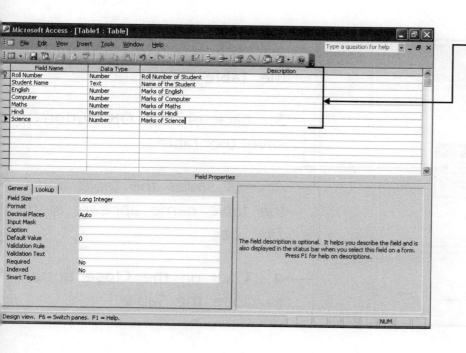

14. Repeat steps 1 — 13 to make the remaining entries in the table to complete it.

Saving and Closing the Table

The next step after creating a table is to save the table in the database. You should give a name to the table before saving it. Once you have saved the table, you can continue working in the Table window or close the window.

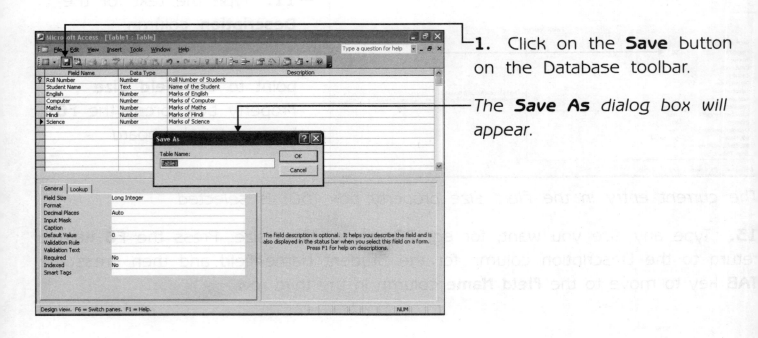

1. Click on the **Save** button on the Database toolbar.

*The **Save As** dialog box will appear.*

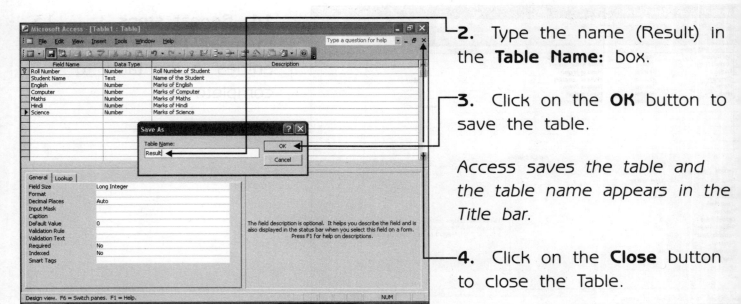

2. Type the name (Result) in the **Table Name:** box.

3. Click on the **OK** button to save the table.

Access saves the table and the table name appears in the Title bar.

4. Click on the **Close** button to close the Table.

Adding Records in a Table

After creating and saving the table, the next step is to add records in the table.

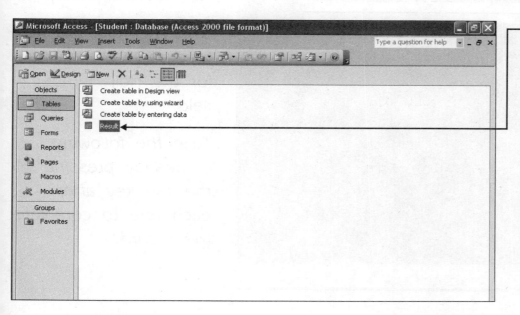

1. Double-click on **Result** in the Student: Database window.

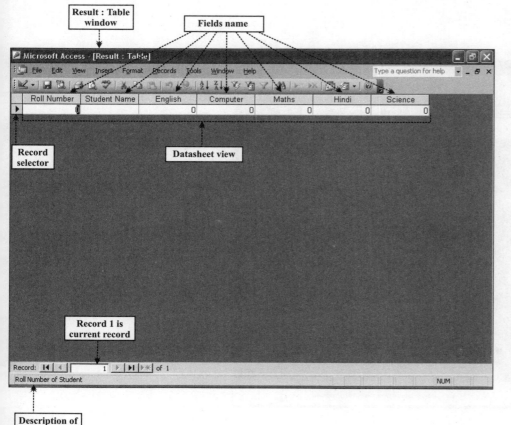

The Result : Table window gets displayed. The window contains the Datasheet view for the Result table.

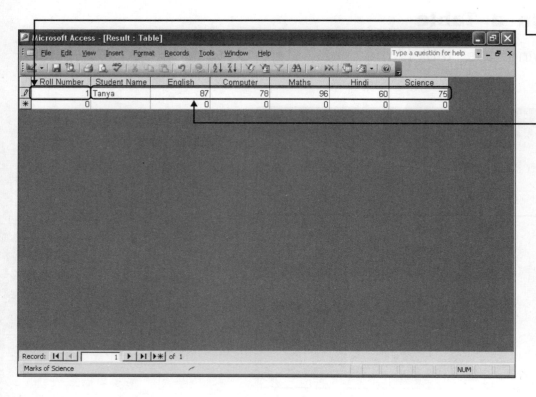

2. Type the Roll Number in the first Roll Number field.

3. Press the **Tab** key to complete the entry for the Roll Number field.

Type the following entries by pressing the Tab key after each one to complete the record.

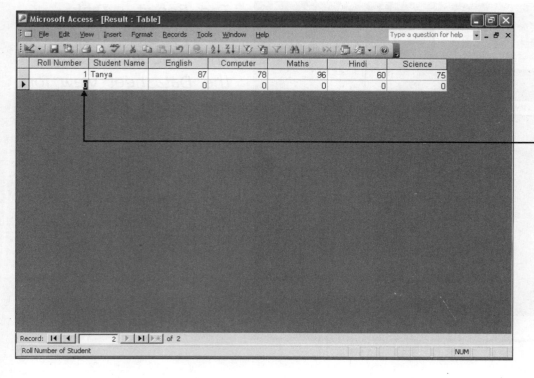

4. After typing the last entry, eg Science, press the **Tab** key.

*The insertion point comes to the **Roll Number** field in the second row.*

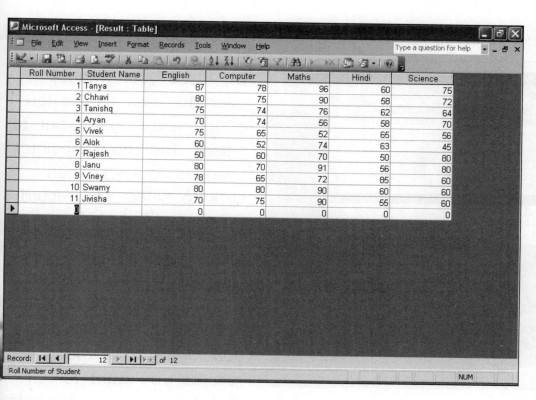

5. Add the remaining records by following the same steps you used to add the first record, as in steps 2 to 4.

Selecting Data in a Table

You can also make selection of data in a table. The selected data appears highlighted on your screen. To make a selection, perform the following steps:

Selecting a Field

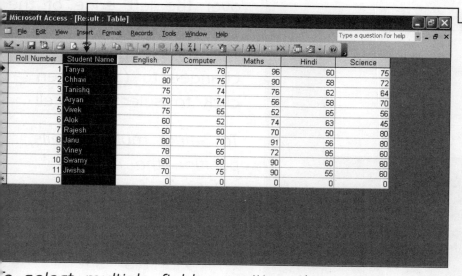

1. Place your mouse over the name of the field you want to select. The mouse pointer changes to (↓). Then click to select the field.

To select multiple fields, position the mouse pointer over the name of the first field. Then drag the mouse pointer (↓) until you highlight all the fields you want to select.

Selecting a Record

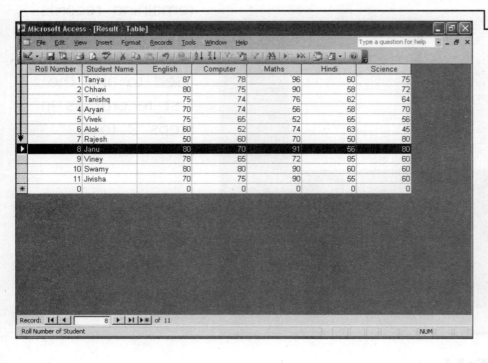

1. Place your mouse over the area to the left of the record you want to select. The mouse pointer changes to (➜). Then click to select the record.

To select multiple records, place your mouse pointer over the area to the left of the first record. Then drag the mouse (➜) until you highlight all the records you want to select.

Selecting a Cell

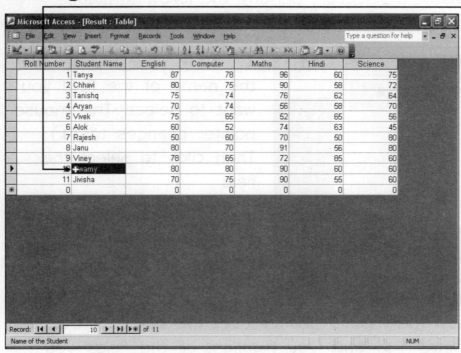

1. Place your mouse over the left edge of the cell you want to select. The mouse pointer changes to (✛). Then click to select the cell.

To select multiple cells, position the mouse pointer over the left edge of the first cell. Then drag the mouse (✛) until you highlight all the cells you want to select.

Rearranging the Fields of Tables

You can change the order of the fields to organize the information in your table systematically.

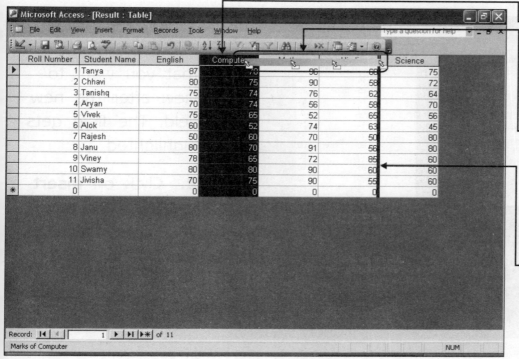

1. Click on the name of the field you want to move. The field gets highlighted.

2. Position the mouse pointer over the field name. Then drag the field to the new location.

A thick line shows where the field will appear.

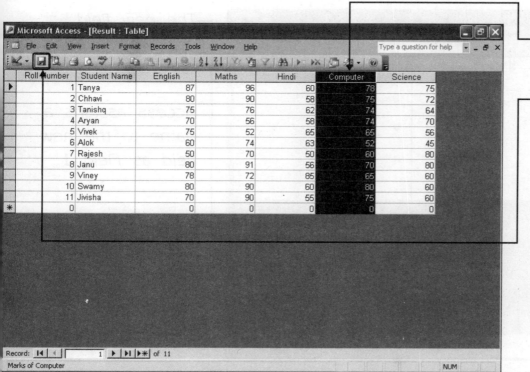

The field appears in the new location.

3. Click on the **Save** button in the toolbar to save the changes you made in the Table.

Adding a Field to the Table

You can add a field to a table when you want to include an additional category of information.

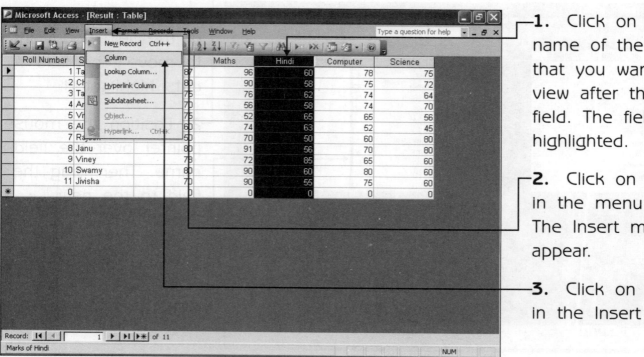

1. Click on the name of the field that you want to view after the new field. The field gets highlighted.

2. Click on **Insert** in the menu bar. The Insert menu will appear.

3. Click on **Column** in the Insert menu.

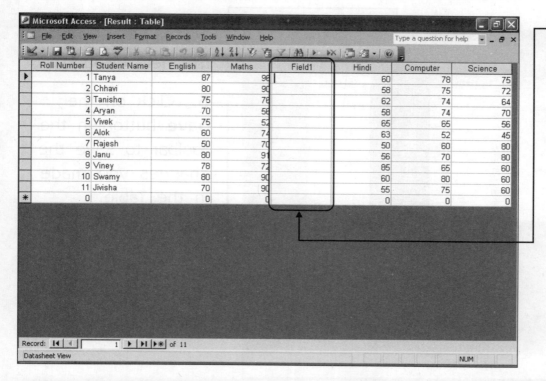

The new field appears in your table.

Access assigns a name to the new field as Field 1.

Adding a Record to a Table

To insert additional information to your table, you can add a new record. For example, you may want to add information about a new customer.

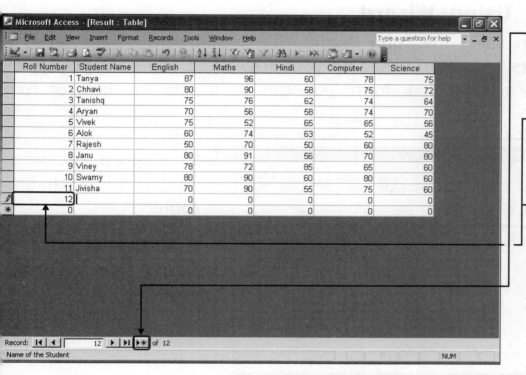

1. Click on (▶⁎) to add a new record to your table.

2. Click on the first empty cell in the row.

3. Type the data that corresponds to the field and then press the Tab key to move to the next cell.

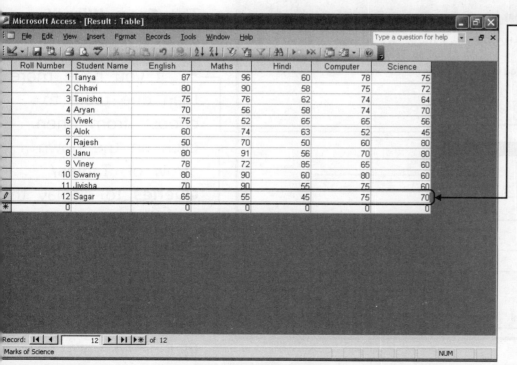

4. Repeat step **3** until you finish entering the data needed for the record.

Access automatically saves each new record you add to the table.

3. Creating a Form

Creating a Form Using Wizard

You can create a form using the **Form Wizard**. The wizard asks you a series of questions and then sets up a form based on your answers. If you want to use the same data from your table in your form, you can do it with the help of Form Wizard.

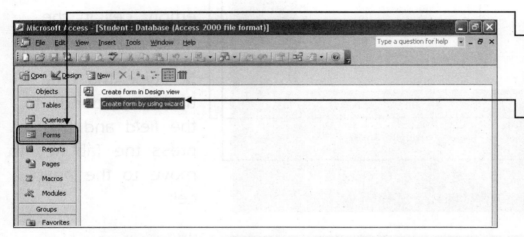

1. Open a database window and click on **Forms.**

2. Double-click on **Create form by using wizard.**

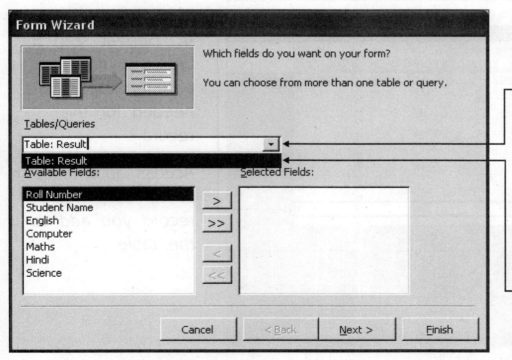

*The **Form Wizard** window appears.*

3. If you have more than one table to choose from, then click on the down arrow of **Tables/ Queries** to display the list of tables in your database.

4. Click on the table that contains the fields you want to include in your form.

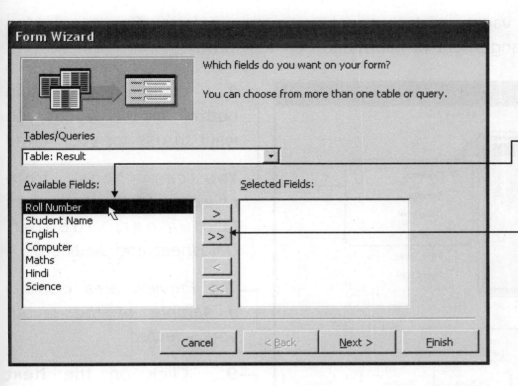

The fields in the table you selected gets displayed in the **Available fields:** area.

5. Double-click on each field you want to include in your form.

To add all the fields at once, click on (>>).

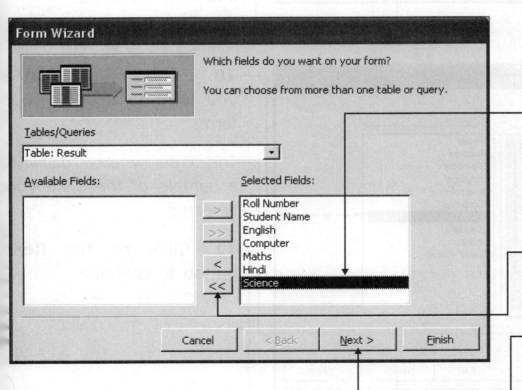

Each field you select appears in the **Selected Fields:** *area.*

6. To remove a field you accidentally selected, double-click on the field in the **Selected Fields:** area.

To remove all the fields at once, click on (<<).

7. Click on the **Next** button to continue.

You can also choose a variety of layouts while creating a form. The layout of a form determines the arrangement of information on the form.

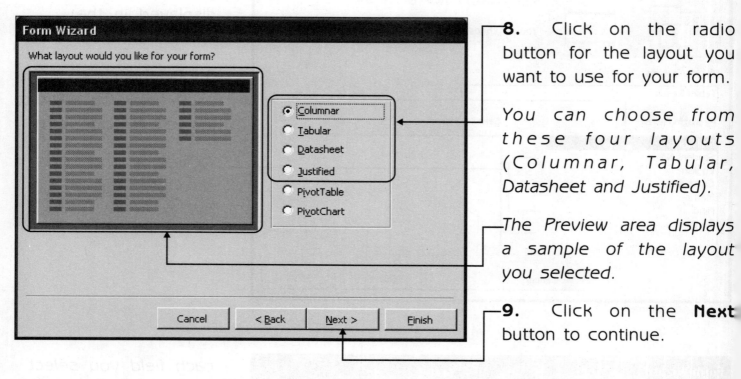

8. Click on the radio button for the layout you want to use for your form.

You can choose from these four layouts (Columnar, Tabular, Datasheet and Justified).

The Preview area displays a sample of the layout you selected.

9. Click on the **Next** button to continue.

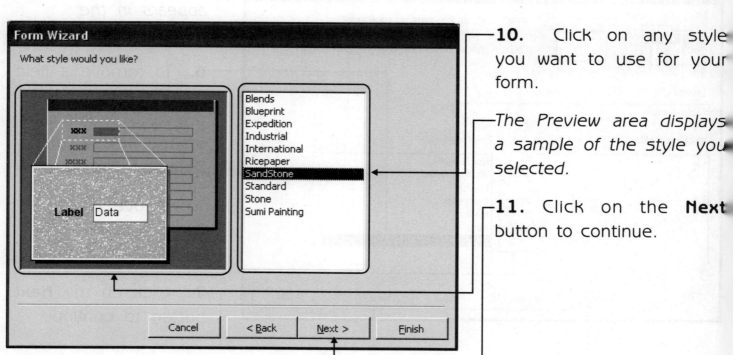

10. Click on any style you want to use for your form.

The Preview area displays a sample of the style you selected.

11. Click on the **Next** button to continue.

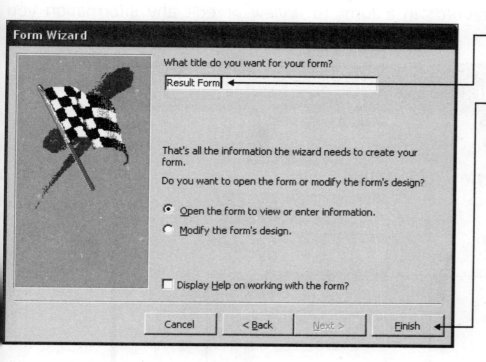

12. Type a name for your form.

13. Click on the **Finish** button to create your form.

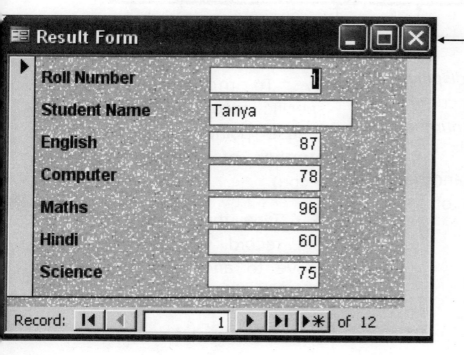

The form appears with the field names you selected.

14. When you finish viewing your form, click on the **Close** button (x) to close the form and return to the Database window.

You can move through the records in a form to review or edit any information you have made.

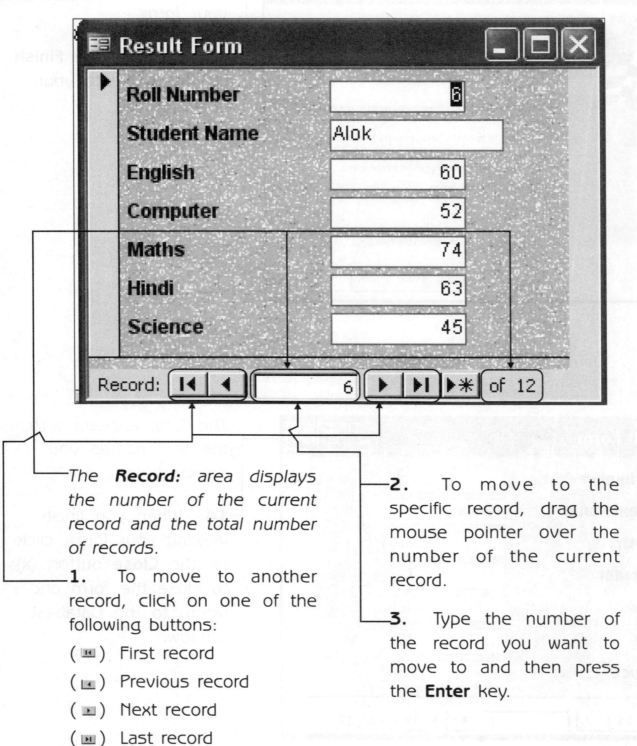

The **Record:** area displays the number of the current record and the total number of records.

1. To move to another record, click on one of the following buttons:

(◄) First record

(◄) Previous record

(►) Next record

(►I) Last record

2. To move to the specific record, drag the mouse pointer over the number of the current record.

3. Type the number of the record you want to move to and then press the **Enter** key.

Editing Data in a Form

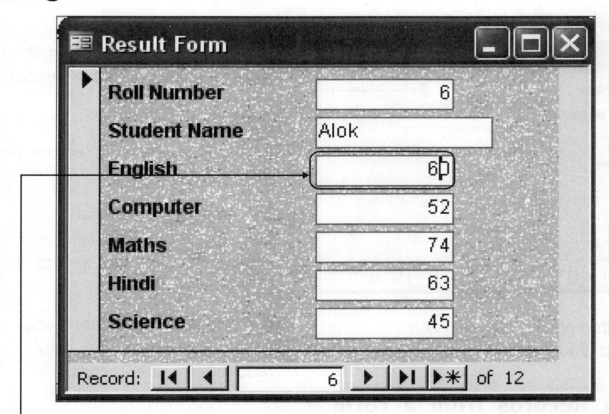

1. Click on the location in the field where you want to edit data.

A flashing insertion point appears in the field.

You can press the arrow keys to move the insertion point.

2. To remove the character to the left of the flashing insertion point, press the **Backspace** key on the keyboard.

3. Type the data where the insertion point flashes on your screen.

Replacing Data in a Cell

1. Drag the mouse pointer over the data until you highlight all the data in the field.

2. Type the new data.

The data you type replaces the previous data in the field.

Adding Records to a Form

You can add a record to your database in your form.

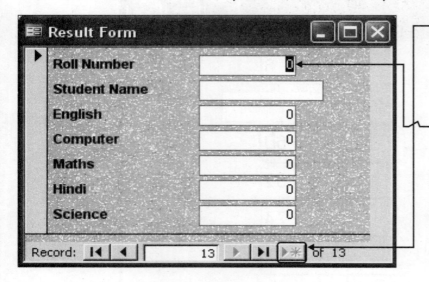

1. Click on (▶*) button in the **Record:** area to add a record.

A blank form appears.

2. Click on the first empty field in the form.

3. Type the data that corresponds to the field and then press the **Tab** key to move to the next field.

Access automatically saves each new record you add using the form.

4. Repeat step **3** until you finish entering all the data required for the record.

Deleting Records from a Form

You can permanently delete a record from your form that is no longer needed.

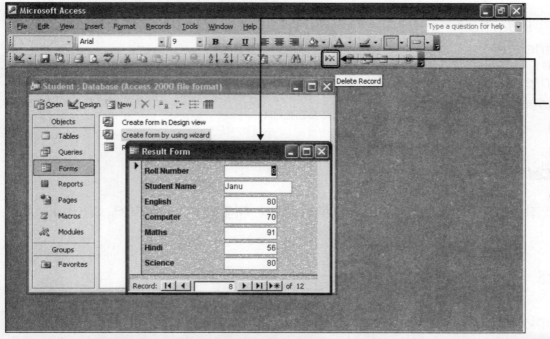

1. Click on the record you want to delete.

2. Click on the **Delete** button (✗) in the database toolbar to delete the record.

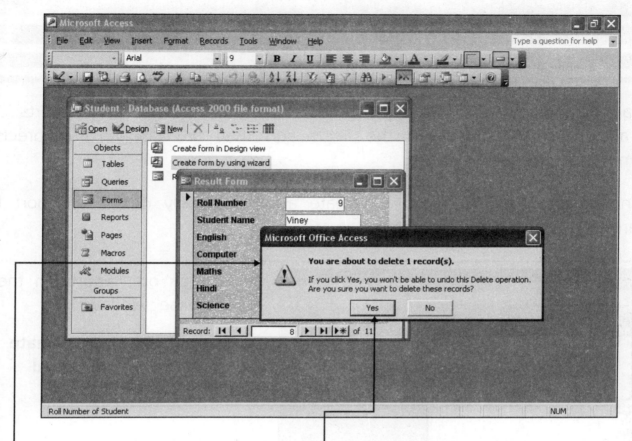

The record disappears from the form.

A warning dialog box appears, confirming the deletion.

3. Click on the **Yes** button to permanently delete the record.

4. Creating a Report

Data can be presented in an organized manner with the help of reports. The report automatically includes all the fields and they are displayed in precisely the same order as in the table.

You can use the **Report Wizard** to create a professionally designed report that summarizes data from your database.

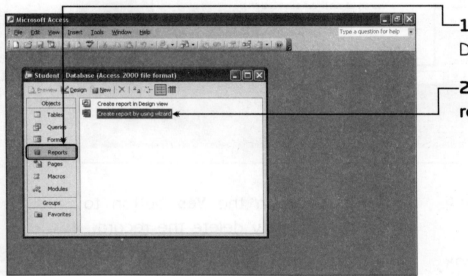

1. Click on **Reports** in the Database window.

2. Double-click on **Create report by using wizard**.

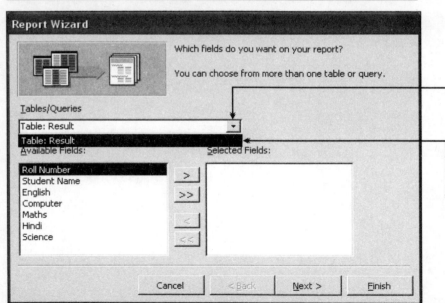

*The **Report Wizard** window appears.*

3. Click on the drop-down menu of **Tables/Queries** to display a list of tables and queries in your database.

4. Click on the table containing the fields you want to include in your report.

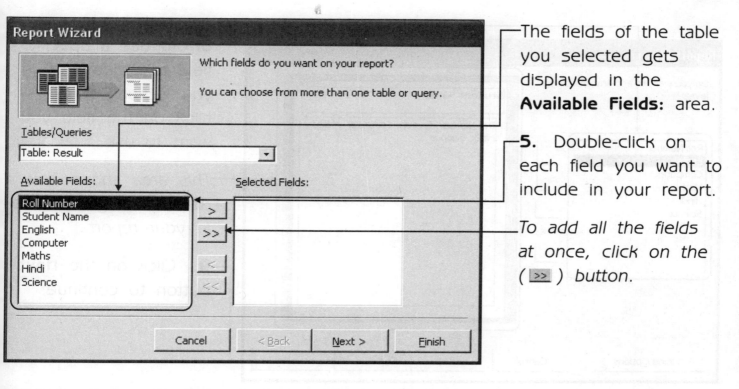

The fields of the table you selected gets displayed in the **Available Fields:** area.

5. Double-click on each field you want to include in your report.

To add all the fields at once, click on the (>>) *button.*

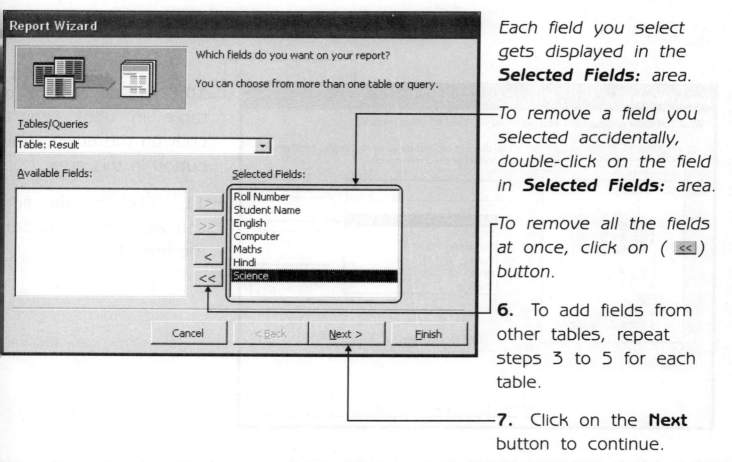

*Each field you select gets displayed in the **Selected Fields:** area.*

*To remove a field you selected accidentally, double-click on the field in **Selected Fields:** area.*

To remove all the fields at once, click on (<<) *button.*

6. To add fields from other tables, repeat steps 3 to 5 for each table.

7. Click on the **Next** button to continue.

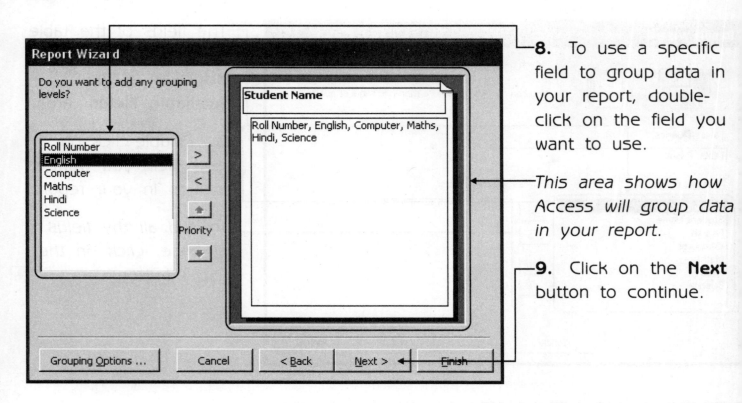

8. To use a specific field to group data in your report, double-click on the field you want to use.

This area shows how Access will group data in your report.

9. Click on the **Next** button to continue.

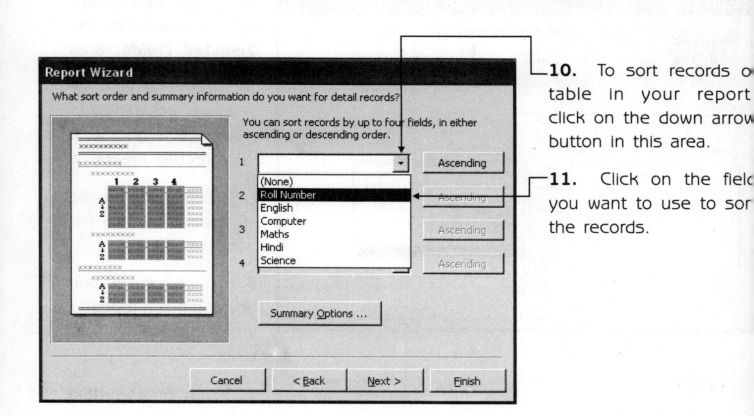

10. To sort records o table in your report click on the down arro button in this area.

11. Click on the field you want to use to sor the records.

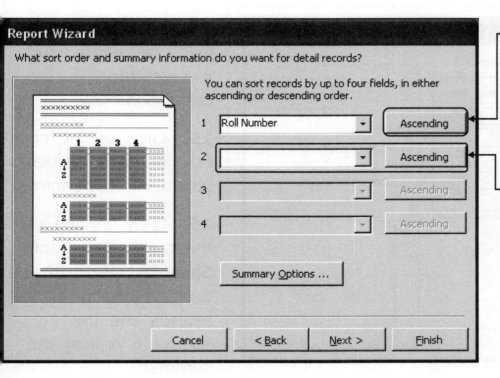

12. Click on this button until it appears the way you want to sort the records. *(Ascending or Descending)*

13. To sort by a second field, repeat steps *10* to *12* in this area.

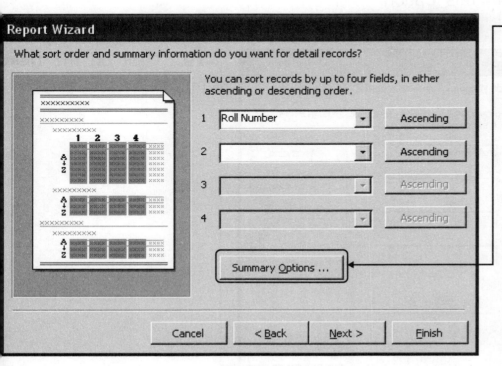

14. To perform calculations in your report, click on the **Summary Options ...** Button.

*The **Summary Options** dialog box appears.*

Summary Options may not be available for some reports. If Summary Options is not available, skip to step 19 to continue creating your report.

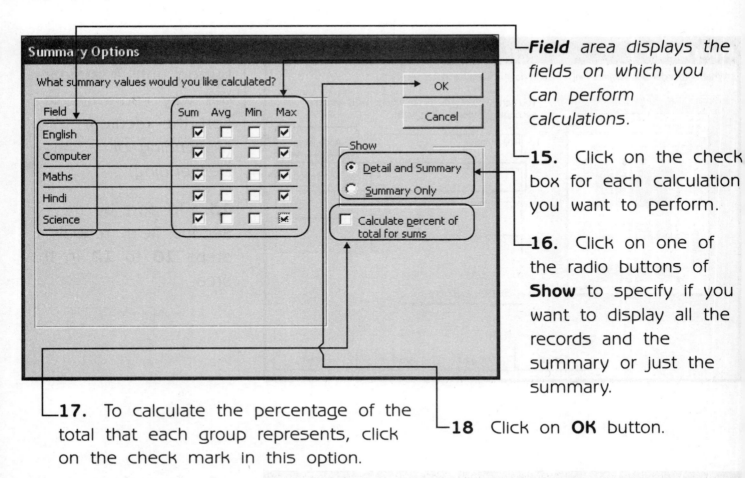

Field *area displays the fields on which you can perform calculations.*

15. Click on the check box for each calculation you want to perform.

16. Click on one of the radio buttons of **Show** to specify if you want to display all the records and the summary or just the summary.

17. To calculate the percentage of the total that each group represents, click on the check mark in this option.

18 Click on **OK** button.

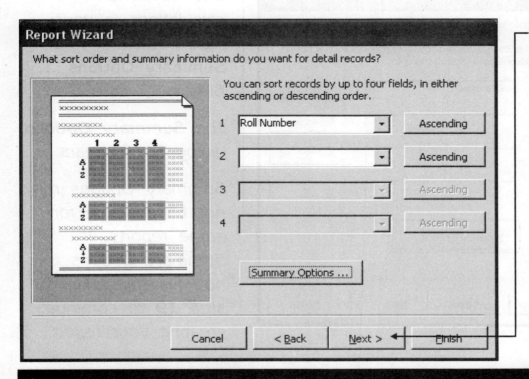

19. Click on the **Next** button to continue.

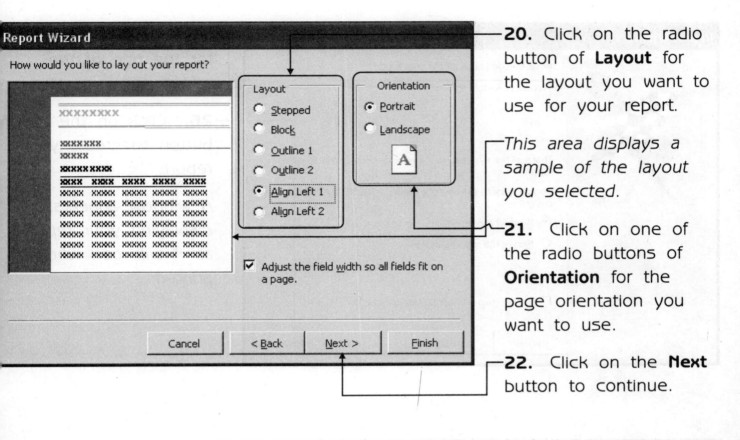

20. Click on the radio button of **Layout** for the layout you want to use for your report.

This area displays a sample of the layout you selected.

21. Click on one of the radio buttons of **Orientation** for the page orientation you want to use.

22. Click on the **Next** button to continue.

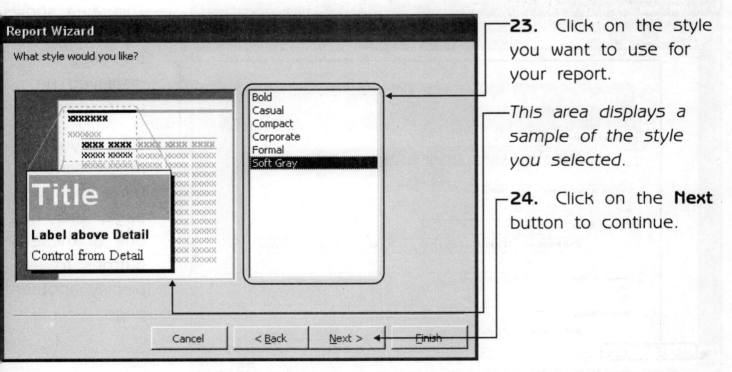

23. Click on the style you want to use for your report.

This area displays a sample of the style you selected.

24. Click on the **Next** button to continue.

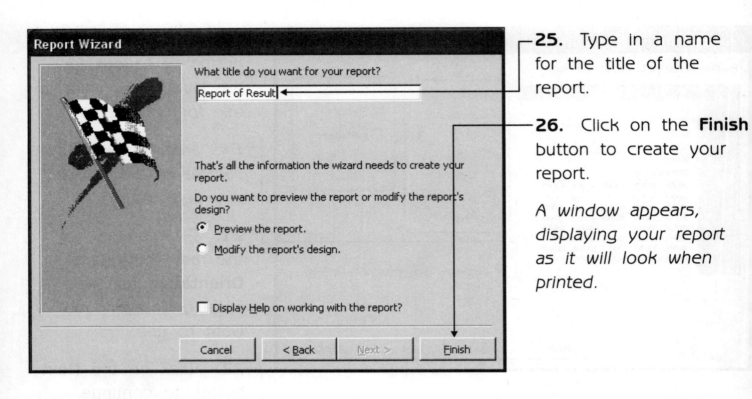

25. Type in a name for the title of the report.

26. Click on the **Finish** button to create your report.

A window appears, displaying your report as it will look when printed.

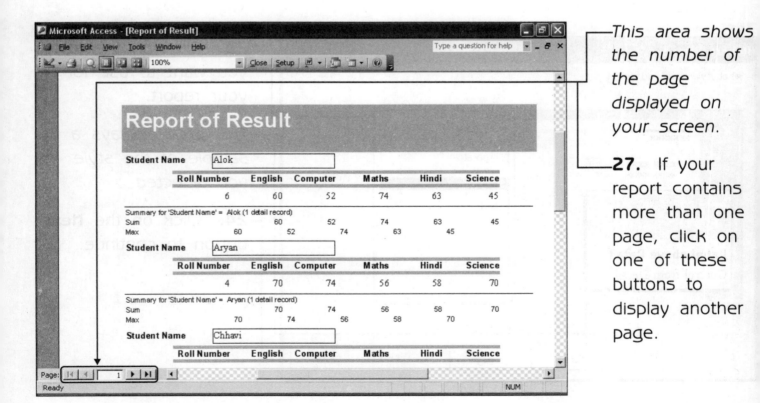

This area shows the number of the page displayed on your screen.

27. If your report contains more than one page, click on one of these buttons to display another page.